Published by Paperview Europe Ltd.

www.paperviewgroup.com

Printed and bound by
Leo Paper Products Ltd.

THE WONDERFUL WORLD OF KNOWLEDGE

FROM STONE AGE TO SPACE AGE

How Your Encyclopedia Works

 Mickey, Minnie, Donald, Daisy, Goofy and Pluto are ready to take you on an adventure ride through the world of learning. Discover the secrets of science, nature, our world, the past and much more. Climb aboard and enjoy the ride.

Look here for a general summary of the theme

Labels tell you what's happening in the pictures

The pictures by themselves can tell you a lot, even before you read a word

Mickey's ears lead you to one of the main topics

Watch out for special pages where Mickey takes a close look at some key ideas

The Solar Sy

The Solar System is th given to our Sun and its fa planets. It also includes th moons, millions of pieces called asteroids and meteo and frozen lumps of dust called comets. Everything can see in the sky is outsi Solar System and is far, far away. Every single star is itself a sun, and each may have its own family of planets and moons.

Saturn is surrounded

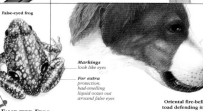

REPTILES AND AMPHIBIANS

Color and Camouflage

Frogs and toads come in nearly every imaginable color, even gold or black. They have a wide range of patterns, from spots and stripes to zigzags.

Color and pattern help frogs and toads survive. Bright colors warn that they may be poisonous. Drab colors camouflage them, or hide them against their background. Many tree frogs are exactly the same green as leaves, while others look like bark. The Asian horned toad has the best camouflage of all. Folds of patchy, brown skin and a flat body make it look like a dead leaf when it lies still on the forest floor.

Folds of brown skin give perfect camouflage

Flat body is hard to see among dead leaves

Asian horned toad

False-eyed frog

Markings look like eyes

For extra protection, bad-smelling liquid oozes out around false eyes

FALSE-EYED FROG
The South American false-eyed frog has large markings on its flanks that look like eyes. These fool some predators into thinking that they are looking at a much larger animal, such as a cat or bird.

COLOR AND CAMOUFLAGE

Dog sniffing curiously at the toad

Strawberry arrow frog

POISON-DART FROGS
Deadly poison oozes from the ski of Central and South American poison-dart frogs. People in the rain forest rub the tips of their arrows and blowpipe darts on the skin of these frogs to collect the poison to use for hunting.

Blue poison-dart frog

Oriental fire-bellied toad defending itself against a dog

Skin oozes a stinging fluid

Bright colored belly

Green and black back

FIRE-BELLIED TOAD
When cornered by a predator, the Oriental fire-bellied toad of eastern Asia arches its back and rears up on its legs to show its fiery underside. Wise attackers back off, because the toad's skin oozes a stinging, bad-tasting fluid.

Toad rears up on its back legs

FIND OUT MORE
MAMMALS: Camouflage
PLANET EARTH: Forests

16

Mickey's page numbers help you look things up. Don't forget there's a glossary and index at the back of each book

Goofy and his friends know how to give you a chuckle on every topic

Mickey points you to more information in other books in your *Encyclopedia*

FIND OUT MORE
THE KINGDOM OF MAMMALS: Camouflage
PLANET EARTH: Forests

Your favourite characters present some facts to astound you and your friends

Numbers lead *you step-by-step through how things happen*

Colourful boxes *zoom in on information*

Mickey's helpers test some ideas themselves

THE SOLAR SYSTEM

HOW OUR SOLAR SYSTEM WAS FORMED

1 The Solar System formed 4.6 billion years ago. It started at the centre of an enormous swirling cloud of gas and dust.

2 The Sun burst into flames and became a star. Its light and warmth spread throughout the new Solar System.

3 Gas and dust left over from making the Sun clumped together in places. These chumps grew bigger and formed the planets.

4 The planets closest to the Sun are small and made from rock and metal. The larger outer planets are made from gas and liquid.

Pluto was the farthest planet from the Sun until 2006, when it was reclassified as a minor planet

Each planet has its own path, or orbit

Planet orbits

ORBITING THE SUN
No matter how still you try to be, you are always moving. This is because the Earth – and all the other planets – are moving. They are flying through Space around the Sun in looping paths called orbits.

Neptune is a cold, blue planet

Uranus is tipped over on its side

THE "PULL" OF GRAVITY
If you throw a ball into the air, it comes down again. The invisible force that pulls it down to Earth is called gravity. The Earth's gravity holds us down on the ground. The Sun's gravity is strong enough to hold all its planets in their orbits.

Gravity pulls a ball to Earth

FIND OUT MORE
PLANET EARTH: Night and day
THE MARVELS OF SCIENCE: Gravity

...is red dust

The Solar System

AMAZING FACTS
★ The Sun is enormous compared to the planets. It is nearly 1,000 times more massive than the giant planet Jupiter.

Contents

INTRODUCING

From Stone Age to Space Age

The human story covers 500,000 years, from the Stone Age to the Space Age. It tells how civilisations began, how empires were built, and it explains how the world has become what it is today.

Early peoples had to make the big discoveries – how to build homes, farm the land, communicate and govern themselves. The world we live in has been built on the work of past generations, and it is still changing today. As each year passes, it becomes another chapter in our amazing history.

The Human Story

The human story begins around 65 million years ago, when animals called primates first appeared on Earth. Over thousands of years, their bodies became apelike, then almost human. Their brains became bigger, and they learned how to use language, light fires and make tools. Modern humans – people like us – developed from these creatures about 100,000 years ago.

HIGHLIGHTS OF THE HUMAN STORY

From around 15,000 B.C. to A.D. 1950 – that is, from the Stone Age to the Space Age – many new civilisations have grown up in different parts of the world. All through history, people's daily lives have continued to change.

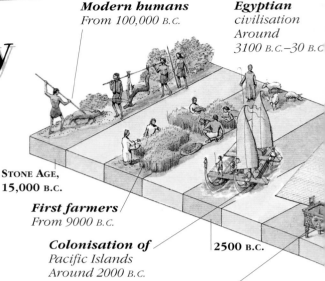

Modern humans
From 100,000 B.C.

Egyptian civilisation
Around 3100 B.C.–30 B.C.

STONE AGE, 15,000 B.C.

First farmers
From 9000 B.C.

Colonisation of
Pacific Islands
Around 2000 B.C.

2500 B.C.

Shang Dynasty
1650 B.C.–1027 B.C.

Muslim Empire
A.D. 700–1400

Khmer Empire
A.D. 802–1402

Silk Road links
Asia and Europe
Around A.D. 1200

Medieval castle
A.D. 1200

Inca civilisation
From A.D. 1440

Benin Empire
A.D. 1400–1900

The Renaissance
A.D. 1400–1550

Formation of the
United States of America
A.D. 1620–1865

French Revolution
A.D. 1789

Timeline of the human story, from the Stone Age to the Space Age

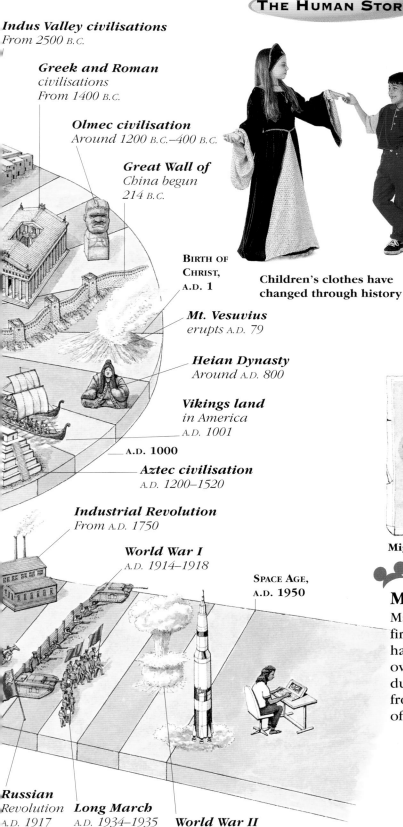

Indus Valley civilisations
From 2500 B.C.

Greek and Roman
civilisations
From 1400 B.C.

Olmec civilisation
Around 1200 B.C.–400 B.C.

Great Wall of
China begun
214 B.C.

BIRTH OF
CHRIST,
A.D. 1

Mt. Vesuvius
erupts A.D. 79

Heian Dynasty
Around A.D. 800

Vikings land
in America
A.D. 1001

A.D. 1000

Aztec civilisation
A.D. 1200–1520

Industrial Revolution
From A.D. 1750

World War I
A.D. 1914–1918

SPACE AGE,
A.D. 1950

Russian
Revolution
A.D. 1917

Long March
A.D. 1934–1935

World War II
A.D. 1939–1945

Children's clothes have
changed through history

MEASURING TIME

Through history, different people have measured time in different ways. Some have used calendars based on the Sun or the Moon. Others have used calendars based on their rulers' reigns. Today, historians often use a Christian calendar, which divides the past into two parts: B.C. (Before Christ was born) and A.D. (Anno Domini – or after Christ was born).

	Year 1	
2000 B.C.	(A.D. 1)	A.D. 2000
(Years counted backward)	(Years counted forward)	

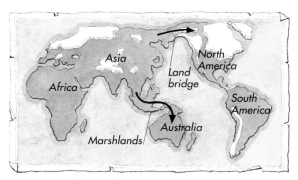

Migration during the last Ice Age, 20,000 B.C.

MOVING AROUND THE WORLD

Many scientists believe modern humans first appeared in Africa. By 20,000 B.C. they had migrated, or travelled and settled, all over the world. They travelled farthest during the Ice Ages, when most seas were frozen in huge ice sheets, leaving bridges of dry land, which people could walk across.

FIND OUT MORE
SPACE: Space Age
GREAT TRAVELLERS AND EXPLORERS:
Migration

The First Farmers

Middle East, 9000 B.C.

☞ The first farmers lived in the Middle East. Around 9000 B.C., people found that grains of wheat and barley dropped on damp ground grew and produced seeds. So they cleared land and planted more seeds. By around 6000 B.C., people in Southeast Asia had discovered how to grow rice. By 5000 B.C. in Central and South America, people were growing potatoes and maize (corn). By 3000 B.C. in Africa, they were growing millet and yams.

FIRST SETTLEMENTS

The first villages grew up arou 9000 B.C., in the Middle East. People left the village to go on hunting expeditions rathe than spend all their lives wandering in search of food.

Early Middle East settlement, 9000 B.C.

FIRST CROPS

It took many years of practice before farmers could be certain of growing good crops. Early farmers harvested wild wheat and barley. Later, this wheat crossed naturally with a kind of grass and produced a new wheat with large, plump seeds.

People used tools called sickles to cut the ripe wheat and barley

Barley

Wheat

Rice

Potatoes

Modern farmers grow the same crops as early farmers

Dogs were the first animals to be tamed, around 20,000 B.C.

12

Houses at Çatal Hüyük

FIRST TOWNS

Jericho in Jordan (built around 8000 B.C.) and Çatal Hüyük in Turkey (built around 6000 B.C.) were the world's first towns. Townspeople lived in houses built of sun-dried mud brick, surrounded by strong walls for protection.

TRADE AND BARTER

Towns and cities were important centres of trade. Farmers brought crops, and hunters brought furs and skins to town markets. Potters, weavers and metal-workers moved to live in towns so they could sell their goods there. Early people did not use money. Instead, they bartered, or swapped, goods they made for others they wanted of equal value.

Eyes were probably made out of semi-precious stones

Carved stone container, from the Middle East (3000 B.C.–2340 B.C.)

Sheep and goats were first tamed and bred by farmers around 9000 B.C.–7000 B.C.

AMAZING FACTS

★ In Çatal Hüyük, the "front door" of most homes was in the roof, for protection. People climbed ladders to get inside their homes.

Early farmers worked hard to harvest crops by hand

Sickles were simple cutting tools with wooden handles and sharp stone blades like rows of teeth

Straw was used for bedding, roofing and floor coverings

FIND OUT MORE
GREAT INVENTIONS: Early tools
PLANTS ARE AMAZING: Farming methods

Ancient Egypt and its Neighbours

Ancient Egypt, 3100 B.C.–30 B.C.

 The nation of Egypt was created in 3100 B.C., when two small kingdoms joined together and began to be ruled by a single king. The people called their king pharaoh, and believed he was a god. Pharaohs ruled Egypt for the next 3,000 years. Egypt became rich and strong, and the pharaohs demanded tributes, or valuable gifts, from weaker neighbouring lands.

FUNERAL PROCESSION

Egyptians believed that people's spirits could only survive after death if their bodies were preserved. So they made mummies by drying bodies in salt and wrapping them in bandages. Mummies of pharaohs and other important people were carried in a procession to their tombs on funeral barge.

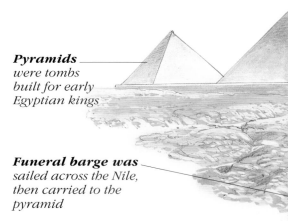

Pyramids were tombs built for early Egyptian kings

Pharaoh's mummy lay inside a casket decorated with gold

Funeral barge was sailed across the Nile, then carried to the pyramid

AMAZING FACTS

★ Not only people were made into mummies. Cats, dogs and falcons were made into mummies, too. Some were pets, mummified to go into the afterlife with their owners.

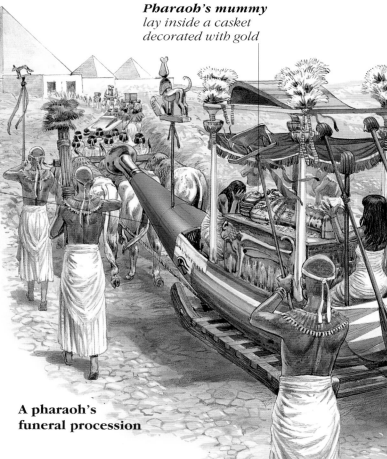

A pharaoh's funeral procession

People from Egypt's neighbouring kingdom of Nubia, Africa, bringing gifts to the pharaoh

EGYPT'S NEIGHBOURS

There were many powerful and rich civilisations close to Egypt. The Sumerians, Babylonians and Assyrians lived in present-day Iraq. The Phoenicians, Canaanites and Hebrews lived on the eastern shores of the Mediterranean. They often traded peacefully, but sometimes they fought one another for land.

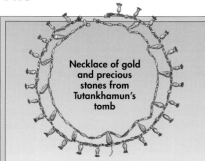

Necklace of gold and precious stones from Tutankhamun's tomb

TUTANKHAMUN'S TOMB

Tutankhamun was a young pharaoh who died around 1350 B.C.. He was buried in a tomb full of treasure in the Valley of the Kings. His tomb remained hidden for over 2,000 years, until it was discovered in 1922.

Farmer using a shaduf *to lift and tip water into ditches running to his fields*

Chest full of treasures, for the pharaoh to use in the afterlife

Weight to balance water-filled bucket

Using a *shaduf* by the Nile

Women mourners were paid to weep and wail

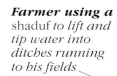

Priests chanted prayers

GIFT OF THE NILE

The Egyptians called their country "the gift of the Nile." Almost every year, the River Nile overflowed its banks, bringing fresh water and rich mud to the dry fields. The farmers needed this "gift" so that their crops would grow.

FIND OUT MORE
FAMOUS PLACES: Great Pyramid
THE WORLD OF ART: Egyptian art

Early India

☞There were many changes during the early part of India's history. From 2500 B.C. to 1500 B.C., the Indus Valley people of northern India lived as farmers. Then invaders, called Indo-Aryans, arrived. Over the next thousand years, the Hindu civilisation developed. It was a mixture of early Indian customs and Indo-Aryan beliefs. India was divided into separate kingdoms, ruled by Hindu warriors. Hindu laws and customs were first written down in holy songs, called Vedas, around 600 B.C..

Kingdom of Ashoka at its height, 260 ▶

Chandragupta's capital city of Pataliputra had strong wooden walls

Lookouts watched for enemies from tall towers

Chandragupta's army setting off to war

Elephants' tusks were tipped with metal

Fierce war elephants trampled enemies underfoot

FIRST INDIAN EMPIRE

Chandragupta Maurya was a Hindu warrior. Before he came to power, India was made up of thousands of small settlements with many languages and customs. By 322 B.C., he had created a new empire that united and controlled much of northern and central India.

INDUS VALLEY CIVILISATION

Around 2500 B.C., two great cities, Harappa and Mohenjo-Daro, were built in the Indus Valley, in present-day Pakistan and northern India. These cities had forts, palaces, open-air baths and comfortable brick houses. The Indus Valley people were farmers, traders, artists and craftworkers, and were ruled by priest-kings.

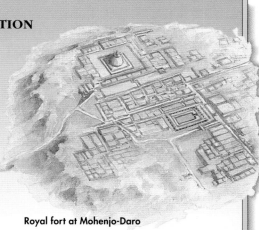

Royal fort at Mohenjo-Daro

Indian soldiers *fought with bows and arrows, and spears*

King Ashoka ordered *pillars carved with his new laws to be built throughout his kingdom*

AMAZING FACTS

★ When the rest of the world managed without indoor plumbing, Indus Valley houses already had bathrooms, piped water and drains.

NEW RELIGIOUS LAWS

King Ashoka was Chandragupta's grandson. He was also a mighty warrior. However, in 262 B.C., after many battles with the Kalinga people, during which 100,000 people were killed, he realised that violence was terrible. He became a Buddhist and made many new laws based on peaceful Buddhist teachings. He also built roads and hospitals.

Ashoka's lion *is a symbol of* *modern India*

RIDING OFF TO BATTLE

From about 320 B.C. to 185 B.C., Hindu warriors fought wars to win riches and conquer new land. They rode to war on elephants and in chariots pulled by horses. The well-trained elephants led the armies into battle.

FIND OUT MORE
THE KINGDOM OF MAMMALS: Elephants
THE WORLD OF ART: Hindu art

First Chinese Empire

☞ For thousands of years, China was divided into separate kingdoms. Then, in 221 B.C., Prince Zheng from the kingdom of Qin conquered the other kingdoms and declared himself Shi Huangdi – First Sovereign Emperor of China. To protect his new empire from warlike nomads who lived on its western borders, he gave orders to build a huge defensive wall – the Great Wall of China.

■ Qin Empire, 221 B.C.
▱ Great Wall of China

AMAZING FACTS

★ When he died, Shi Huangdi was buried with over 6,000 lifesize terra cotta warriors to protect him and guard his tomb.

Officers rode in chariots pulled by horses

Foot soldiers fought with spears and halberds – sharp bronze blades fitted to long poles

WARRING STATES
The period from 481 B.C. until 221 B.C., during which China was divided into rival kingdoms, is called the time of the Warring States. Prince Zheng was able to defeat the other rival states because his army was strong and well organised.

Imperial Guard of the Qin army

Hole in centre so that coin could be kept on a string

Qin bronze coin, 220 B.C.

NEW LAWS

When Prince Zheng became emperor, he made many changes to bring his empire under his control. He made new laws and appointed new officials. He also made coins, weights and measures the same throughout China, and planned new roads and bridges.

BEFORE THE EMPIRE

The earliest Chinese dynasty, or ruling family, we know about was the Shang. It ruled from about 1650 B.C. to 1027 B.C.. Shang people lived by farming and were skilled metalworkers. The first Chinese writing was invented in Shang times.

Shang bronze vessel, used for offerings to ancestor spirits

Chinese scholar writing with a brush

BURNING OF THE BOOKS

Shi Huangdi ordered writings that did not agree with his own ideas to be burned or destroyed. In this way, he hoped to unite his empire. He also tried to destroy the writings of Kong Zi (Confucius), one of China's most important thinkers.

Soldiers on horseback (called cavalry) carried bows, swords and spears

Crossbowmen used crossbows to fire short, heavy arrows, called bolts

Soldiers wore tunics of padded cotton, leather and iron plates

FIND OUT MORE
FAMOUS PLACES: Great Wall of China
FAMOUS PEOPLE: Kong Zi

Mediterranean World

Roman Empire at its height, A.D. 200

Between 800 B.C. and A.D. 500, the land around the Mediterranean Sea was home to two great civilisations. The Ancient Greeks were sailors, farmers, and craftworkers who lived in small, independent city-states. They were most powerful between 500 B.C. and 350 B.C.. The Ancient Romans were great soldiers, builders and engineers. By A.D. 200, they ruled an empire stretching from Germany to North Africa and the Middle East.

CITY OF ROME
Rome, in Italy, was the busy, noisy, crowded capital city of the Roman Empire. By A.D. 300, over 1 million people lived there. Emperors and rich citizens made their homes in splendid villas and palaces. Ordinary families lived in simple apartment buildings.

BURIED CITY
Pompeii was a wealthy city south of Rome. In A.D. 79, it was buried under mud and ash when the nearby volcano of Vesuvius erupted. Most of the people were killed by poisonous gas. However, the layers of ash preserved the buildings and contents, which have since been uncovered.

Plaster casts of people killed in Pompeii

City of Rome,
A.D. 200

Forum –
meeting place
and market

Basilica –
government offices
and law courts

Imperial
palace

Theater of Marcellus –
thousands of people
came here to watch plays

Capitoline Hill –
site of a great temple
to Jupiter, king of the
Roman gods

Cattle
market

Helmet

Shield

Body armour

Woolen
tunic

Sword

Spear

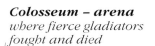ndals

Roman
foot soldier

ROMAN ARMY

Roman soldiers were the best
trained in the world and had the
best weapons. They built long,
straight roads to march along,
and walls and forts to defend
the Roman Empire from attack.

Colosseum – arena
*where fierce gladiators
fought and died*

Aqueduct – raised
*channel bringing
fresh water from the
mountains to Rome*

ACROPOLIS OF ATHENS

Athens was the most powerful city-state
in Ancient Greece. The people of Athens
led Greek armies to fight against Persian
invaders in 480 B.C.. The Persians
attacked the Acropolis, a rocky fortress
in the centre of Athens, but the Greeks
drove them away. Later, the people of
Athens built many splendid new temples
on the Acropolis.

Erechtheum –
*temple of an ancient
hero-god*

Parthenon –
*dedicated to
Athene, the city's
guardian goddess*

Acropolis
of Athens,
450 B.C.

Temple of Nike
(Victory)

AMAZING FACTS

★ The Romans invented
the first real concrete –
by mixing water, pebbles
and volcanic ash.

Circus Maximus –
*track where
exciting chariot
races were held*

FIND OUT MORE
PLANET EARTH: Volcanoes
SPORT: Olympic Games

Investigating the Past

Archeologists – people who study the past – have different ways of finding out how people lived long ago.

Archeologists can read old documents or study the ruins of ancient buildings. They can also use modern scientific techniques such as CAT scans and powerful microscopes to see inside a mummy's bandages or examine tiny grains of pollen from plants grown long ago. Sound waves can find things buried deep underground, X-rays can reveal ancient weapons inside lumps of rust, and computers can reconstruct ruins.

On a Dig

Archeological excavations – called digs, for short – help us find out about the past. Diggers remove layers of soil, one at a time, to reveal ancient remains. Jewelry, leather and fragments of cloth tell us what people wore. Weapons tell us how people fought and died. Cooking pots and rubbish tips tell us what people ate, and even if they were ill.

Photographs are taken of wall paintings and other remains

Archeologists make maps and plans of the site

Grids are put over part-buried objects, then photographed to show how big they are

Sieve to sift rock and sand in search of bits of pottery or coins

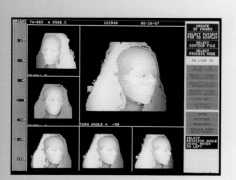

Computer CAT scan picture of the head of Tabes, a female mummy from Ancient Egypt

THE WRITTEN WORD

Buildings and objects tell us how people lived, but writing can tell us even more – how and what people thought, and what they believed. People from different civilisations have used many kinds of writing. Historians have managed to decode and understand most of them, but some still remain unread.

Mayan glyph, or picture writing

Early Chinese writing on an oracle bone from the Shang Dynasty

Recording an Aboriginal story in Australia

THE SPOKEN WORD

Most people in the past could not read or write. So they trained their minds to remember important information and ancient stories, and passed them on by word of mouth. Today, the spoken word can still be a very useful source for historians investigating the past.

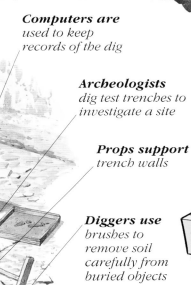

Computers are used to keep records of the dig

Archeologists dig test trenches to investigate a site

Props support trench walls

Diggers use brushes to remove soil carefully from buried objects

A dig on the island of Crete, Greece

Soft brushes are used to uncover buried objects

FIND OUT MORE
COMMUNICATIONS: Writing
HOW MACHINES WORK: CAT scans

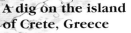

Dark Age Europe

In Europe, the years from A.D. 500 to A.D. 1000 are often known as the Dark Ages, because there were so many wars. Viking raiders burned and looted villages and farms. Parts of southern and eastern Europe were also attacked, by invaders from central Asia and the Middle East. But the Dark Ages were also full of excitement. Explorers travelled great distances and built new settlements, and kings encouraged learning, trade and art.

Scandinavia – home of the Vikings

VIKING SETTLERS

Not all Vikings were raiders. Farming families left Scandinavia in search of better land. They settled in Scotland, Ireland, Russia, France, England, Iceland and Greenland. In A.D. 1001, they settled in North America, but left it after a few years.

Vikings built fast, sleek wooden longships

Wooden houses *had roofs made of pieces of grassy turf*

Viking village in Scandinavia

CELTIC WARRIORS

The Celts were warriors from central Asia, who settled in northwestern Europe from around 750 B.C.. They were farmers, hunters and skilled metalworkers. Celtic tribes in France and Germany were defeated by the Romans around 50 B.C., but remained powerful for hundreds of years longer in Ireland, Scotland and Wales.

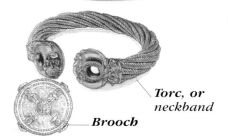

Torc, or neckband

Brooch

Celtic jewelry

Viking ships often had a dragon's head carved at the front

Decorated page from a Christian book

EARLY CHRISTIANITY

The Christian faith began in the Middle East, during the lifetime of Jesus Christ (A.D.1 to A.D. 33). During the next 700 years it spread through Europe. Many cathedrals and churches were built. Christian monks produced beautiful religious books.

Viking merchants travelled long distances to trade

KING OF THE FRANKS

Charlemagne was king of the Franks. He founded a vast empire in northern Europe and forced conquered peoples to follow the religion of Christianity. He aimed to create a new Roman Empire and had himself crowned Holy Roman Emperor in A.D. 800.

King Charlemagne ruled from A.D. 768 to A.D. 814

AMAZING FACTS

★ Celts often placed the skull of a defeated enemy above their front door, to protect their house from evil spirits.

FIND OUT MORE
TRANSPORT: Ships
GREAT TRAVELLERS AND EXPLORERS: Vikings

25

The Muslim Empire

Muslim Empire around 800

 Muslims are people who follow Islam, a faith preached by the Prophet Muhammad who lived in Arabia from A.D. 570 to A.D. 632. After Muhammad's death, Islam was spread to many parts of the world by Muslim traders, and by Muslim soldiers setting out to conquer new lands. By A.D. 800, the Muslim Empire was rich and powerful. It stretched from southern Spain to western China and had many fine cities and towns. The empire was ruled by leaders called caliphs.

CAPITAL CITY

Baghdad, in present-day Iraq, was the capital of the Muslim Empire. It was founded by Caliph al-Mansur in 762. The city was built in a circle. Palaces, mosques and colleges were in the centre. Schools, hospitals and workers' homes were around the outside.

Libraries contained thousands of books and manuscripts

Decorated page from the Qur'an

MUSLIM LAW

Throughout the Muslim world, people were governed by laws based on the Muslim holy book, called the Qur'an. People of other faiths were treated fairly, but they had to pay extra taxes.

Centre of the city of Baghdad, c. 765

ARTS AND CRAFTS

Workers throughout the Muslim Empire were skilled at many crafts, including pottery, tile-making, glassblowing, metalworking and carpet-weaving. They made beautiful objects to decorate mosques, palaces and homes. European and Asian merchants travelled to Muslim trading cities to buy Muslim crafts and to sell furs, silks and spices.

AMAZING FACTS

★ Babur, the first Mughal emperor, won his first battle when he was just 14 years old.

★ Baghdad had over 65,000 public baths.

Plate

Water jug

Delicate Muslim tableware

Mosque, where Muslims worshipped, with domes and minaret towers

Astronomers used astrolabes to plot the position of the stars

Mughal emperor Shah Jahan at court

MUSLIM WARRIORS

The Mughals were Muslim warriors who came from central Asia. They ruled India from 1526 to 1858. The Mughal emperors gave money generously to encourage art, architecture and learning. The Mughals created a new, Mughal civilisation in India, which mixed Muslim styles of art and architecture with those of early India.

Colleges and schools were founded to study astronomy, science and medicine

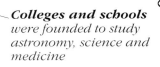

FIND OUT MORE
FAMOUS PEOPLE: Leaders of Islam
THE WORLD OF ART: Islamic art

Central and South America

☞ The Americas were home to many great civilisations, including the Olmec, Toltec, Maya, Aztec and Inca. The Maya were most powerful from A.D. 250 to A.D. 900, and the Aztecs and Incas ruled large empires from around 1440 to the early 1500s. The people from these civilisations created vast cities, huge temples and wonderful works of art. Each civilisation had its own languages, laws and customs.

■ Maya Empire at its height, 350
■ Aztec Empire at its height, 1500
■ Inca Empire at its height, 1525

AZTEC SACRIFICE

The Aztecs feared that one day the world would end. To prevent this, they believed they had to feed the gods with human blood. So they went to war to capture prisoners and killed them as human sacrifices to the gods.

Great Temple and shrines *of Tlaloc (god of rain) and Huitzilopochtli (the Aztecs' tribal god) where people were sacrificed*

Stone ri *fixed to t*

PLAYING GAMES

The Aztecs' favorite sport was a ball game called tlachtli, or pot-a-tok. Two teams tried to hit a solid rubber ball through a stone ring fixed to a wall. It was a fast, rough game. Only nobles could play, and on special festival days, losing teams might be sacrificed to the gods.

Players sometimes *wore padding to protect their arms and knees*

Tlachtli game in the Aztec city of Tenochtitlán, c. 1500

ARTS AND CRAFTS

Central American peoples were skilled craftworkers. They carved beautiful statues and made fine pottery, fabrics, jewelry, masks and feather headdresses. The Maya people also made folding books, called codices, full of picture writing.

Figure of the Aztec god Chacmool – used to hold a human sacrifice's heart

Olmec jade carving

Terraced fields were *cut into steep mountain-sides to plant crops*

Temple of Tezcatlipoca, *"Smoking Mirror," dedicated to one of the Aztecs' chief gods*

Spectators cheered *on their team at the game*

Ball courts could be *up to 60 m (197 ft) long and 10 m (33 ft) wide*

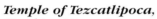

Rope bridge across *a mountain gorge*

Inca mountain village

MOUNTAIN LIFE

The Incas ruled a vast empire in the Andes mountains of South America from around 1400 to 1533. They built cities with palaces and temples, and thousands of kilometres of roads. People lived by farming maize and potatoes, and by keeping llamas for their wool.

AMAZING FACTS

★ The Aztecs made the world's first chocolate, from pounded cocoa beans, water, honey and spices.

★ The Maya were skilled mathematicians. They were the first people to invent a sign for "zero."

FIND OUT MORE
COMMUNICATIONS: Inca couriers
FAMOUS PLACES: Tikal

Medieval Europe

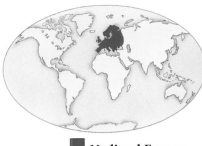

■ **Medieval Europe**
□ **Wales**

During medieval times, from around 1000 to 1500, Europe was ruled by kings and queens. The kings and queens relied on lords, knights and church leaders to help them. In return, kings and queens gave them land. The landowners were very rich. They could afford splendid castles, good food and fine clothes. Their lands were farmed by ordinary people who gave the landowners a share of the food they produced, and sometimes money, in return for a small cottage and a tiny plot of land.

Chapel tower –
for religious services

King's tower –
containing the
royal bedrooms

MEDIEVAL CASTLE

The earliest castles, built around 1000, were made of wood and earth. From around 1200, people built massive stone fortresses with thick walls. Towns grew up around castles and fortresses for protection.

Thick stone wall
protected the castle and
surrounding buildings

Conwy Castle, Wales,
built between 1283
and 1287

AMAZING FACTS

★ A knight's full battle armour was so stiff and heavy that he needed help from a trainee knight, called a squire, to put it on.

30

KNIGHTS AND LADIES

Knights were soldiers who fought on horseback. It was their duty to help kings defend their lands. Usually, knights came from noble families, but a very brave soldier might be knighted as a reward. Knights were expected to be courteous to women. Some ladies let a knight carry a scarf or glove as a token of their loyalty.

Medieval painting showing the love of a knight for his lady

Great Hall – for feasts for important guests

Prison tower with an underground dungeon

FIGHTING FOR THE HOLY LAND

The Crusades were wars fought between Christians and Muslims over the right to rule the Holy Land – the area around the city of Jerusalem. The Crusades began in 1096, when Christian soldiers marched on Jerusalem, and ended in 1291, when Muslim armies drove the Christians out of the Holy Land.

European knights capturing Jerusalem on the First Crusade in 1099

POWER OF THE CHURCH

The Christian church played an important part in medieval European life. It was very rich and powerful and controlled most hospitals, schools and colleges.

Monk writing a manuscript in a medieval monastery

Outer gateway with a drawbridge, guarded by soldiers

FIND OUT MORE
DANCE, DRAMA AND MUSIC: Pageants
FAMOUS PLACES: Castles

Tang and Song China

The Tang emperors ruled China from 618 to 907. They conquered new lands, rebuilt important cities, such as Chang'an (now Xi'an), and encouraged trade. When the Tang empire collapsed, China split into five warring kingdoms. The Song dynasty took power in 960 and brought back peace. Tang and Song emperors valued art and science, and at this time, scientists invented many useful things, such as printing, the compass and rockets.

Tang Empire, 618–907

CITY OF CHANG'AN

During the Tang era, the city of Chang'an was the capital of China. Over 1 million people lived there, including the emperor and his officials, rich nobles, merchants and scholars.

AMAZING FACTS

★ The Silk Road was over 7,000 km (4,375 miles) long. It took months, or even years, for a merchant to travel from one end to the other.

Lookouts kept *watch on top of each gate*

Farmers carried pigs, *chickens and vegetables in horse-drawn carts to sell at city markets*

Heavy goods, such as rice, *were ferried to Chang'an by boat, along waterways*

City of Chang'an in Tang times

Chinese painting of Mongol nomads, 14th century

WANDERING MONGOLS

The Mongols were nomads, who roamed across the grasslands of northern and central Asia. The Mongols attacked northern China during Tang and Song times. In 1206, they united under a warrior called Genghis Khan and began to conquer many lands.

EAST MEETS WEST

Chang'an and the city of Kaifeng lay toward the eastern end of the Silk Road – a network of pathways that linked important trading cities in the East and West. Merchants from Europe and the Middle East travelled to China along the Silk Road, bringing gold, linen cloth and leather to trade for silk.

Song merchants selling silk

Houses were built of wood, with thatch or tile roofs

Chang'an was surrounded by strong walls made of earth and bricks

Tang porcelain jug

AIMING FOR PERFECTION

Porcelain – very fine, smooth, shiny pottery – was invented in China about 1,800 years ago. During Tang and Song times, workers experimented with many new pottery styles to create the most beautiful pottery ever seen.

FIND OUT MORE
FAMOUS PLACES: Chang'an
FAMOUS PEOPLE: Genghis Khan

Japan, Korea and Southeast Asia

The lands of Japan and Southeast Asia have different landscapes, climates, traditions and beliefs. But from around 1150, they all became famous for wonderful buildings and works of art. The Khmer rulers of Cambodia declared themselves god-kings and ordered huge temple-cities to be built as their homes. In Indonesia, kings from the Sailendra and Srivijaya dynasties created huge Buddhist temples, such as Borobudur on Java.

JAPANESE COURT LIFE

Life at the Japanese court was elegant and gracious, but governed by strict rules. Taking part in traditional ceremonies, having good manners and showing respect were all very important. At court, women usually sat apart from visitors – except their family and close friends – behind delicate screens made from painted paper or wood.

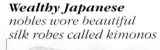

Wealthy Japanese nobles wore beautiful silk robes called kimonos

Japanese court at Heian-Kyo (present-day Kyoto), c. 800

AMAZING FACTS

★ Fashionable Japanese women painted their faces white and their teeth black. Teeth were blackened because the white make-up made them look yellow.

Khmer *farmers grew rice*

Farming by the city of Angkor Wat, Cambodia

KOREAN DYNASTY

In 668, the Silla Dynasty in Korea took control of several smaller kingdoms to make one powerful state. In 918 the Koryo Dynasty took control. Because of its geographical position, Korea became an important link between China and Japan.

Korean *sowan,* or academic building

Delicate paper screen, *decorated with paintings of mountains and trees*

Japanese men *wore their long hair in a topknot*

Servants bowed *low as a sign of respect*

KHMER EMPIRE

In 802, Khmer King Jayavarman II began a mighty empire in Cambodia that flourished for over 600 years. The Khmers' most famous temple-city, Angkor Wat, was built between 1113 and 1150. Armies from Thailand invaded the empire in the 1400s and forced the Khmers to leave Angkor.

Carving of ship on Borobudur temple, island of Java, Indonesia

MALACCAN STRAITS

All traders wishing to buy spices from Indonesia had to sail through the Straits of Malacca – a narrow channel between the Indonesian island of Sumatra and the Malaysian peninsula. From around 800, the straits were controlled by Buddhist kings. After 1400, they were ruled by Muslim sultans.

FIND OUT MORE
FAMOUS PLACES: Borobudur
GREAT TRAVELLERS AND EXPLORERS:
Khmer Empire

Australia and the Pacific Islands

Australia and New Zealand – home of the Aboriginal people and Maoris

Australia was unknown to Europeans until 1645, but people from Southeast Asia first arrived and settled there around 50,000 years ago. It took thousands of years to settle all the Pacific Islands. People from New Guinea travelled to live in Fiji around 1300 B.C.. From there, settlers went to Tonga and Samoa. Their descendants finally reached Hawaii and New Zealand around A.D. 800.

Ancestor spirits were carved over the doorway to protect the people inside

Wooden fence was used for protection

Maori jade *hei-tiki*, or pendant

LIVING IN NEW ZEALAND

The Maoris were the first people to settle in New Zealand. They were fierce warriors and lived by farming, hunting and fishing. The Maoris built wooden houses in large, fortified villages.

Wooden fish carving from the Solomon Islands

Chiefs and warriors had tattooed faces

Spear decorated with feathers, used for fishing and fighting

Cloth cloak and kilt made from the linen plant, flax

SKILLED CARVERS

The Pacific islanders were skilled at carving wood, shell, whalebone and volcanic stone. The Maoris made beautiful carvings out of a hard, green stone called jade.

Maori gateway to village, New Zealand

SAILING THE PACIFIC

Pacific islanders were expert boat builders. They sailed great distances across the vast Pacific Ocean in outrigger canoes, steering by the Sun and the stars. They made maps of sea routes between well-known islands out of twigs, shells and stones.

Sail made from woven palm leaves

Canoes loaded with pigs, chickens and seeds of food plants

Outrigger canoe

FIRST AUSTRALIANS

Life in the harsh Australian climate was hard. Aboriginal families (the first people in Australia) lived in shelters made of animal hides and branches. They hunted kangaroos and birds, dug for roots and grubs, gathered seeds and caught shellfish.

Modern-day Aboriginal people in Australia

AMAZING FACTS

★ The Pacific Island people invented surfing. Their homelands had wonderful beaches and huge ocean waves.

★ Maori sea-fishing nets were about 800 metres (half a mile) long.

FIND OUT MORE
CHILDREN OF THE WORLD: Australasia
GREAT TRAVELLERS AND EXPLORERS: Navigation

African Empires

Africa has been home to many great civilisations, each with its own customs, languages and gods. Some were based around big, busy cities, such as Cairo and Tangier. These were ruled by Muslims who built palaces, colleges and mosques. Other civilisations, like the kingdoms of Ghana (700–1200) and Mali (1200–1500) grew rich by raising cattle and mining gold. City-states such as Kilwa and Mogadishu on the east coast traded slaves and ivory with India and Arabia.

■ Africa
☐ Kingdom of Benin

POWERFUL EMPIRE

Benin was a kingdom in west Africa, in present-day Nigeria. Its people lived by farming, but they were also famous warriors and metalworkers. Benin was ruled by powerful kings called obas, and the kingdom remained strong from 1400 to 1900.

Wood-burning furnace
for melting bronze for statues

Bellows were used to
blow air onto the fire
to keep it burning hot

BENIN BRONZES

Benin craftworkers made head-shaped statues and decorated square panels, called plaques, of brass and bronze. The statues were placed on family altars, to remember dead ancestors. The plaques were used to decorate the royal palace.

Younger workers
were trained by
senior craftsmen

**Benin craftworkers making
bronze statues, c. 1600**

ASHANTI GOLD

The Ashanti people lived in present-day Ghana from 1600 to 1900. Their kings controlled the biggest gold mines in Africa. The Ashanti metalworkers made beautiful gold statues and heavy jewelry.

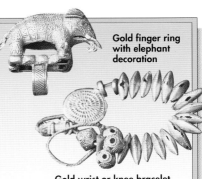

Gold finger ring with elephant decoration

Gold wrist or knee bracelet

CENTRE OF LEARNING

The city of Timbuktu, in present-day Mali, was a famous centre of learning and had many colleges. It was built close to camel routes across the Sahara Desert and became rich through trade.

The Muslim mosque at Timbuktu

Thatched roof *sheltered workers from the hot sun*

Houses had *thatched roofs*

Only men made *statues – Benin women were weavers, farmers and traders*

Walls to protect *houses and grain store*

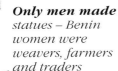

Rich people bought *statues to place on family altars*

Enclosure *for cattle*

City of Great Zimbabwe

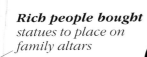

AMAZING FACTS

★ The Sultan of Kilwa was very rich. Around 1430, he built a palace of coral with over 100 rooms and a swimming pool.

★ Around A.D. 900 in East Africa, a goatherd noticed his goats didn't sleep after nibbling wild coffee berries. This was how coffee – which can keep people awake – was discovered.

WALLED CITY

Kings of the Shona people, from present-day Zimbabwe, built a walled palace-city, called Great Zimbabwe, around 1200 to 1400. The Shona people kept cattle, and traded in leather, gold, copper and ivory.

FIND OUT MORE
THE WORLD OF ART: Bronze-casting
GREAT TRAVELLERS AND EXPLORERS: Slavery

North American Civilisations

At one time there were over 300 different Native American tribes living in North America. They spoke many different languages, and had very different lifestyles, depending on where they lived. But there were also likenesses between the different peoples. They all found ways of surviving in difficult environments and had a great respect for nature. They all were skilled at art and crafts, and they were proud of their ancient customs and traditions.

North America – home of the Native American tribes

IROQUOI VILLAGE

The Iroquoi people lived in the eastern woodlands of the prese. day U.S. from 1600 to 1800. The villages were made up of severa wooden longhouses. The peopl lived by hunting and farming.

Houses were about 45 m (150 ft) long

About 12 families lived in each longhouse

Iroquoi villagers building longhouses, c. 1650

Iroquoi villagers planted fields of maize (corn), beans and squash (pumpkins)

Cree

Teepee

Igloo

Inuit

Paiute

Sectoan

Mud-brick *house*

Dakota

Wooden *longhouse*

Pueblo

Creek

Some Native American tribes and their homes

LAND AND HOMES

The Native Americans' way of life varied according to where they lived. In the woodlands, people lived in wooden houses and hunted deer, moose or bears. On the plains, they lived in teepees, or tents, made out of animal skins, and hunted buffalo. In the hot south they built homes out of sun-baked mud bricks, and farmed corn, trapped rabbits or gathered seeds.

JOINING TOGETHER

The Iroquoi League was an alliance of five native peoples – the Mohawk, Seneca, Oneida, Onondaga and Cayuga. They joined together from around 1570 to 1780, to fight their enemies and, later, the European settlers.

AMAZING FACTS

★ The Inuit people from the north invented the first sunglasses – goggles of wood or bone that protected their eyes from blinding sunlight reflected off ice and snow.

Longhouses were *made of wooden poles* *covered with strips of* *elm-tree bark*

MAKING ART

Native Americans used many different kinds of materials, from semi-precious stones called turquoise to a rock called mica, to make useful and beautiful things.

Today we can wear jewelry made by the descendants of ancient Native American tribes

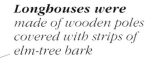

Spiral *pattern for* *decoration*

Pottery jug made by the Anasazi people of New Mexico, c. 1100

FIND OUT MORE
THE WORLD OF ART:
Native American art

Europe
France

Renaissance and Revolution in Europe

The years from around 1400 to 1800 saw great changes in Europe. These began with the Renaissance, which changed the way many people saw the world. Next came new religious ideas, which caused bitter quarrels between Protestants and Roman Catholics, and sometimes war. Bad rulers and a huge difference between the lives of rich and poor people led to revolution – first in France, then in other European countries.

REVOLUTION!

The French Revolution broke out in 1789, as a protest against bad government, heavy taxes, poverty and shortages of food. Rioters attacked royal palaces, set up a new government and killed the king and queen. Thousands of people were executed by a machine called the guillotine.

Florence, Italy – a centre of Renaissance art and learning

REBIRTH OF LEARNING

In Europe, the years from 1400 to 1500 are often called the Renaissance, which means rebirth. Scholars, scientists and artists experimented with new ideas, which spread through printed books.

Execution by guillotine during the French Revolution

Supporters of the revolution wore red, white and blue badges in their hats

REFORMING THE CHURCH

From around 1500 to 1600, there were quarrels among Christians in Europe. Groups of Christians called Protestants left the Roman Catholic church to set up new churches. They wanted to read the Bible and say prayers in their own languages, rather than in old-fashioned Latin. They also questioned many Roman Catholic beliefs.

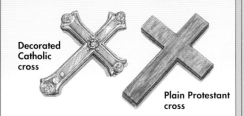

Decorated Catholic cross

Plain Protestant cross

COURT LIFE

European kings and queens believed that God had given them the right to rule, and they refused to let ordinary people take any part in ruling their country. Rulers lived shut away in magnificent palaces, and wore splendid clothes and jewels. After revolutions and riots in many countries in Europe, rulers started to make changes to improve the lives of their people.

Empress Maria Theresa, ruler of Austria from 1740 to 1780

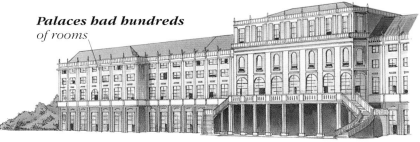

Palaces had hundreds of rooms

Schönbrünn Palace, near Vienna, Austria, home of Empress Maria Theresa

Blade

The guillotine killed people by cutting off their heads with a sharp blade

AMAZING FACTS

★ Over 3,000 people were guillotined during just one year of the French Revolution, between 1793 and 1794. This time was called "the Terror."

Enemies of the revolution were taken to the guillotine in open carts

FIND OUT MORE

FAMOUS PLACES: Palaces
THE WORLD OF ART: Renaissance

Trade Around the World

The first voyage around the world was made by Portuguese sailors from 1519 to 1521. Once European explorers found that it was possible to sail to distant countries, such as Africa, India, or America, European traders soon followed them.

European customers were eager to buy all kinds of new things from faraway lands, such as Chinese porcelain and Indian cotton cloth. Trade also resulted in an exchange of ideas between people of different countries and cultures.

SOUTHEAST ASIAN TRADE

For centuries, merchants from eastern Africa, Arabia, India and China sailed to busy trading ports in Indonesia. They bought cloth and spices. From around 1500, European sailors also began to trade in Southeast Asia.

European ships *had deep wooden hulls to store lots of cargo*

European merchants *bargained to get the best prices*

Batik cloth from Indonesia is still traded for spices from India and Southeast Asia

Cotton, silk, spices and *tea from India, Southeast Asia and China*

Avocados, potatoe: *chilis, tomatoes, mai and cocoa from Nor and South America*

Goods traded around the world

Otomi Native Americans meeting Spanish sailors

NEW WORLD TRADE

From 1492, Spanish and other European sailors crossed the Atlantic to North, Central and South America, which they called the New World. They found gold, silver and new foods, such as maize, potatoes and tomatoes.

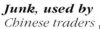

Cargo ship, used by European merchants

Junk, used by Chinese traders

Dhow, used by merchants from Arabia, India and East Africa

Outrigger canoe, used by Pacific islanders

Trading boats and ships from around the world

Spice-growers carried their goods to warehouses at big ports

SAILING ACROSS THE SEAS

Until the mid-19th century, all ships were built of wood. They had sails made of cloth or matting to catch the wind. Small ships also had oars or paddles for sailors to use in shallow water or when the wind dropped. Sea travel was slow, and it could take many months to sail from Asia to Europe.

Trading at the port of Atjeh, Indonesia, c. 1550

ALL ALONE

Japan and China did not want foreign traders in their countries. They banned overseas visitors except from special trading ports, such as Nagasaki in Japan and Guangzhou in China.

Special trading port in Guangzhou, China, 1830s

FIND OUT MORE
TRANSPORT: Sailing ships
GREAT TRAVELLERS AND EXPLORERS: Spice trade

Formation of the United States

The United States, 1898

The first European settlers arrived in North America around 1540. They built churches, villages and farms. For the next 200 years, European countries claimed the right to rule America, until the people who lived there rebelled. During this time, the settlers and Native Americans sometimes lived peacefully side by side. At other times, there was war. From around 1800, more settlers arrived and most Native Americans were driven from their lands.

GO WEST

From the 1850s, thousands of people travelled west across America. The journey was long and dangerous, and life in the western settlements was hard but people hoped to find land they could farm

Armed rider looked out for unfriendly Nativ Americans or bandits

Wagons were pulled by horses, mules, or oxen

Settlers travelling west by wagon train

46

MAYFLOWER SETTLERS

In 1620, a small group of families, called the Pilgrims, left England to settle in eastern America. They wanted to start a new community, ruled by laws based on the Bible. They named their new village Plymouth, after the port in England from which they had sailed.

The *Mayflower,* the Pilgrims' ship

AMERICAN INDEPENDENCE

Britain ruled 13 colonies in America. In 1776, the colonies drew up a Declaration of Independence, stating their right to form a new nation, the United States of America. This started a seven-year war. The colonies defeated the British in 1783.

Colonial leaders signing the Declaration of Independence, 4 July 1776

Tops of wagons were made of canvas stretched over a hoop frame

Men rode or walked beside the wagons; sick people, women and children usually rode inside

Front wheels were smaller than back wheels, to help with steering

THE CIVIL WAR

In the southern states of America, black slaves from Africa worked on cotton plantations. The northern states wanted to ban slavery. North and south also quarreled over government and trade. They finally fought in a Civil War, which lasted from 1861 to 1865. The north won, and the slaves were freed.

Northern (Union) soldiers

Southern (Confederate) soldiers

AMAZING FACTS

★ Between 1900 and 1910, almost 9 million settlers left Europe and eastern Asia to live in the United States.

FIND OUT MORE

CHILDREN OF THE WORLD: United States
GREAT TRAVELLERS AND EXPLORERS: United States

Industrial Revolution

England – birthplace of the Industrial Revolution

During the Industrial Revolution, there were great changes in the way people worked. These changes began in Britain around 1750, when inventors designed machines to spin thread and weave cloth more cheaply and quickly than small spinning wheels and hand-weaving looms. By 1850, new machines were producing many other goods in factories. This new way of working soon spread to other parts of Europe and to the United States.

London in the late 1800s

NEW FACTORY TOWNS

Factories were built close to supplies of coal and water, which were needed to work the new steam-powered machines. The towns that grew up around the factories were dirty and crowded.

AMAZING FACTS

★ Between 1820 and 1860 over 7,000 km (4,375 miles) of railway tracks were built in Europe to carry goods to shops and ports.

WORKING UNDERGROUND

The Industrial Revolution could not have happened without coal. But often it was mined at a terrible price. Men, women and children worked long hours in bad conditions. Many were hurt or killed in rock falls, explosions and fires.

Children opened and closed wooden trapdoors when a truck passed through

Lighting came from bare candle flames

Miners pulled heavy coal wagons to the surface

FACTORY WORKERS

Many poor families left the countryside to work in the new factories. They hoped to find well-paid, regular work. However, factory work was hard. The working hours were long, and the big machines were dangerous to run. Workers' homes were often overcrowded, and diseases spread easily.

Many women went to work in the new cloth mills

AGRICULTURAL REVOLUTION

From around 1700, landowners in Europe began to experiment with new scientific ways of growing crops and breeding animals. Later, new farm machines, such as reaping machines, were invented to make harvesting crops easier and much more efficient.

Sheep and cattle were bred to produce more wool, milk and meat

Reaping machines, pulled by horses, harvested crops

Wooden props *held up the tunnel roof*

Miners dug coal *by hand with picks and shoveled it into sacks*

Inside a coal mine, c. 1800

FIND OUT MORE
HOW MACHINES WORK:
Farming machines, Production machines

Two World Wars

During the 1900s, there were two terrible wars. These wars are called world wars because so many countries were involved.

World War I lasted from 1914 to 1918. It started because Britain and France wanted to stop Germany taking control of Europe. People called it "the war to end all wars" because so many soldiers died. However, just 21 years later, a second world war began. This lasted from 1939 to 1945. It started when Adolf Hitler, the ruler of Germany, ordered the invasion of other European countries.

ON THE FRONT LINE

In Western Europe during World War I, armies dug rows of deep trenches along the front line – the ground where enemy soldiers met face to face. The trenches were meant to protect troops from gunfire, but they soon filled up with water and dead bodies, and many soldiers died from disease.

Exploding shells fired by enemy guns

Spy plane flying overhead

Doctors and nurses worked in hospitals behind the lines

Battlefield in Western Europe, during World War I

Flooded trenches became full of mud

Stretcher bearers dodged bullets to rescue injured soldiers

Only male first-aid workers were allowed on the battlefield

Adolf Hitler watching a Nazi rally, 1933

WORLD WAR II

Hitler's supporters were called Nazis. The Nazis killed many Jews and other groups of people in Europe before they were defeated in 1945. Japan and Italy were allies of, or sided with, Hitler. Britain, France, Russia, Canada, Australia, New Zealand, South Africa and the U.S. fought against their armies. China, with Britain and the U.S., stopped Japan conquering most of Southeast Asia.

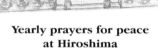

White doves are released as a symbol of peace

The Red Cross, set up *in 1863, won the Nobel Peace Prize in 1917 for helping the injured during the war*

Many soldiers *were badly injured by poison gas*

Yearly prayers for peace at Hiroshima

MONUMENT FOR PEACE

After World War II, a peace monument was built in the Japanese city of Hiroshima. It remembers the 150,000 people who were killed or injured when the world's first atomic bomb was dropped on Hiroshima by the U.S. Air Force on August 6, 1945. Each year, people meet there to pray for peace.

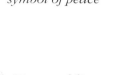

FIND OUT MORE
ATLAS OF THE WORLD: World map
FAMOUS PEOPLE: Alfred Nobel

Communist Revolutions

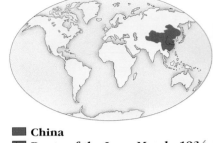

■ China
■ Route of the Long March, 1934–

Communism is a way of ruling a country that aims to give power to ordinary people. During the 1900s, there were communist revolutions in many countries, including Russia (in 1917) and China (in 1949). The communists got rid of kings and landowners, and set up cooperatives in which people shared the land and what they produced.

THE LONG MARCH

From 1934 to 1935, Chinese communists, led by Mao Ze Dong, made a daring escape from land surrounded by their enemies. They marched about 9,600 km (6,000 miles) through wild countryside, from southeast to northwest China. The communists took control of all China in 1949.

Over 100,000 Chinese communists set out on the Long March

CONTROLLING THOUGHTS

The Cultural Revolution was part of the Communist Revolution. It was started by Chinese communist leader Mao Ze Dong in 1966. He wanted to control how people lived, worked and thought. Until 1976 (when Mao died), schools and colleges were closed, and experts and teachers were sent to work on farms.

Red Guards studied Mao's "Thoughts," written down in a little red book

The Cultural Revolution was spread by Red Guards – young people with strong communist ideas

Young communists during the Cultural Revolution

AMAZING FACTS

★ Part of the Long March took place in bitter winter weather, and the marchers had little food. Conditions were so grim that only one in ten marchers survived.

The Long March
took over a year

Marchers crossed
lands held by their enemies and risked being attacked

Communist revolutionary leader Lenin, making a speech in Red Square, Moscow, November 7, 1918

THE RUSSIAN REVOLUTION

In 1917, Russian communists, workers and soldiers started violent protests in the city of St. Petersburg. The protesters wanted a new government that would treat them fairly. In 1918, communists killed the Russian royal family. This started a civil war. The communists won in 1922, and Russia became a new communist nation called the U.S.S.R. – the Union of Soviet Socialist Republics. Since 1991, the U.S.S.R. has split up into 15 countries.

THE COLD WAR

From 1945, the U.S.S.R. and the U.S. became enemies. The U.S.S.R. believed in state control and communism. The U.S. believed in business and freedom of speech. This division was called the Cold War – a war without fighting. The countries "fought" by building up nuclear weapons and supporting wars in smaller nations, such as Cuba (1961–62) and Vietnam (1964–75). The Cold War ended in 1989.

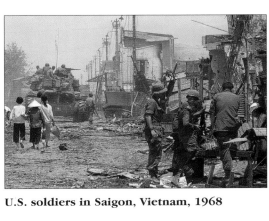

U.S. soldiers in Saigon, Vietnam, 1968

FIND OUT MORE
CHILDREN OF THE WORLD:
China, Russia

Communists on the Long March, 1934–35

Our Changing World

Human lives have changed all through history, but the greatest changes have happened in recent times.

Before World War II, some European countries ruled colonies all over Southeast Asia, Africa, Central and South America, the Caribbean and the Pacific. Since 1947, many of these colonies have become independent and govern themselves. In some countries, independence was only won after a bloody struggle, and life for some of the new nations has been hard.

NATIONAL CELEBRATIONS

In Southeast Asia, Burma (now called Myanmar) became independent from Britain in 1948. Singapore and Malaysia won independence in 1957. These and many other new nations have celebrations, called National Days, every year to mark when they became independent.

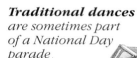

Some government buildings were built when the British ruled Singapore

National Day celebrations in Singapore, held every year on 9 August

Traditional dances are sometimes part of a National Day parade

Newspapers tell us what is going on all around the world

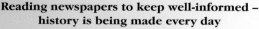

Reading newspapers to keep well-informed – history is being made every day

NEW PROBLEMS

Many new nations have faced problems. They have had to build new roads, factories, hospitals and schools. Some have had to face droughts or floods. Sometimes, rival leaders have quarreled and there have been periods of civil war. However, the new nations have survived and some have become rich through trade.

The Singaporean flag was created when the country became independent

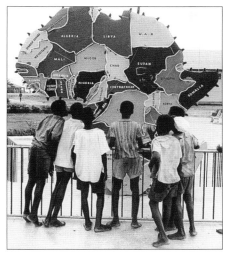

Children from newly independent Ghana looking at a map of countries in Africa, 1957

Members of the government watch the National Day parade

PEACEKEEPING

The United Nations (U.N.) was set up in 1945 to keep international peace and to try to solve problems without fighting. Today, most independent countries are members of the U.N..

Older people may remember the time before their country became independent

U.N. peacekeeping soldiers in Somalia, Africa, 1992

Children enjoy taking part in National Day celebrations

BECOMING INDEPENDENT

Since 1947, when India and Pakistan became independent from Britain, many nations have become independent and rule themselves.

Raising the Indian flag on independence day, 1947

FIND OUT MORE
FAMOUS PLACES: United Nations
FAMOUS PEOPLE: Leaders of nations

Glossary of Key Words

Ancestor: A member of a person's family or race who lived many generations before.

Astrolabe: An instrument once used by scientists and sailors to measure the position of the Sun and the stars in the sky.

Astronomer: A scientist who studies moving objects in Space.

Buddhist: A person who follows the teachings of Buddha, a religious leader who lived from c. 563–483 B.C..

c. or circa: An approximate date, for example, C. A.D. 1000 means about A.D. 1000.

CAT scan: A machine that produces detailed images of the inside of the body using computer technology.

Christian: A follower of the teachings of Jesus Christ, a religious teacher who lived in the Middle East c. AD 1–33.

Citizen: A person born in a country, or accepted as a member of that country, who has to obey its laws and is protected by them.

Civilisation: A society with its own laws, customs, beliefs and artistic traditions.

Civil war: A war between people who live in the same country.

Colony: A settlement or country governed by another country.

Conquer: To overcome or take control of a place by force.

Custom: A way of behaving that a particular group of people has had for a long time.

Dungeon: An underground prison.

Empire: A group of countries, states, or peoples ruled over by an emperor, empress, or other powerful leader.

Excavation: An area of land that is dug up to uncover objects or buildings from the past.

Fortress: A strong building, usually occupied by soldiers, used to protect people or an area from attack.

Gladiator: An Ancient Roman who fought, often to the death, against another man or a wild animal in a public arena.

Hindu: A person who follows Hinduism, a religion based on sacred writings from Ancient India.

Independent: An independent country is one that is ruled by its own government.

Manuscript: The original copy of a book or document, often written by hand.

Medieval times: Also known as the Middle Ages. The historical period from about A.D. 501–1500.

Minaret: A tower that is part of a mosque, from which people are called to prayer.

Monastery: A place where men called monks live in a religious community.

Muslim: A person who follows Islam, a religion based on the teachings of the Prophet Muhammad, who lived in Arabia c. A.D. 570–632.

Noble: A person with a title, such as a Duke, or from a high-ranking family.

Nomad: A person who moves from place to place with the seasons, and who has no fixed home.

Nuclear weapon: An extremely powerful explosive weapon such as an atomic bomb.

Olmecs: People who settled on the east coast of Mexico from about 1200–400 B.C..

Plantation: A kind of farm where one type of crop, such as sugarcane, coffee, or cotton, is grown in large quantities. In the past, plantations were often worked by slaves.

Preserve: To protect from damage or rotting, for example the mummification of a body.

Religion: A group of beliefs that tries to explain all things and that usually accepts that there is a god or gods controlling all life.

Revolution: An extreme and far-reaching change in the way that something is done, such as in the Industrial Revolution, or in the government of a country, such as in the Russian Revolution.

Sacrifice: An offering of a plant, animal, or human life to the gods.

Scholar: Someone who spends their life studying and learning.

Sovereign: A supreme ruler, such as a king, queen, or sultan.

Sultan: The sovereign of an Islamic country.

Tax: Money paid to a government or ruler to help run a country.

Terra cotta: A brownish red clay that can be baked to make pots.

Toltecs: People who established an empire in Mexico during the period from about A.D. 900–1100.

Tribe: A group of people descended from the same ancestors, and often with the same leader.

Index

Acknowledgments

AUTHOR
Fiona MacDonald

CONSULTANT FOR FROM STONE AGE TO SPACE AGE
Jane Shuter BA (Hons), PGCE has written several books
about history, covering a wide range of subjects. Living in
the UK, she has also acted as a history consultant and
edited various publications.

EDUCATIONAL CONSULTANTS
Lois Eskin, BSc, is a publishing consultant with special expertise
in organisational planning, research and product planning for
educational publishers.
Kurt W. Fischer, PhD, Professor at Harvard University,
Graduate School of Education.

INTERNATIONAL CONSULTANTS
Pamela Katherina Decho, BA (Hons), is a consultant editor
specialising in Latin America.
Zahara Wan is a consultant editor specialising in Southeast Asia.
Minghua Zhao, PhD, MSc, MA, BA, is a consultant editor
specialising in China and East Asia.

ILLUSTRATORS
Stephen Conlin, Peter Dennis, Luigi Galante, Christian Hook,
Andre Hrydziusko, John James, Nicki Palin, Eric Robson,
Mike Saunders, Michael Welply, Paul Wright. Disney art colouring:
Neil Rigby. Disney art inking: Alessandro Zemolin

FOR DISNEY ARTWORK IN THIS BOOK
Fernando Guell
With special thanks to Michael Horowitz and Carson Van Osten

AGENCY PHOTOGRAPHS
13 Werner Forman Archive (WFA)/Toni Ralph Collection, New
York; 15 WFA/E.Strouhal; 17 Ann & Bury Peerless; 19 Sheridan/
Ancient Art & Architecture Collection; 20 Corbis/Bettmann;
22 Alexander Tsiaras/Science Photo Library; 23 WFA/National
Museum of Anthropology, Mexico; 25 E.T.Archive; 26 & 27 Robert
Harding Picture Library; 29l N J Saunders,29r WFA/British
Museum, London; 31l E.T.Archive/British Library, 31r E.T.Archive/
Bibliotheque Nationale, Paris; 33t The Bridgeman Art Library,
33b Robert Harding Picture Library; 35 Werner Forman Archive;
36t WFA courtesy Entwistle Gallery, London, 36b WFA/British
Museum, London; 39 WFA/Asantehene of Kumasi; 41 WFA/
Maxwell Museum of Anthropology Albuquerque,NM; 42 Jonathan
Blair/Corbis; 45t E.T.Archive, 45b The Bridgeman Art Library;
47 Museum of the City of New York/Corbis; 48 The Bridgeman Art
Library; 51 Peter Newark's Military Pictures; 53t Topham
Picturepoint, 53b Tim Page/Corbis; 55t Rex Features Ltd,
55b Chris Rainier/Corbis:

CHILDREN'S PHOTOGRAPHS
Ray Moller

PROJECT MANAGEMENT FOR DISNEY
With special thanks to Cally Chambers

PROJECT MANAGEMENT FOR PAPERVIEW
Isabelle Demolin, Delphine Prinselaar

COVER DESIGN
Louise Laurent